Enough

Carole Richard Thompson

FUTURECYCLE PRESS

Mineral Bluff, Georgia

Published by FutureCycle Press
Mineral Bluff, Georgia, USA

ISBN 978-1-938853-28-9

To Norm, my darling boy
who brings our morning coffee
and sits on the side of the bed with me.

Table of Contents

The House of Cards

There is a tiny house that sits askew,
holding out, holding on.
Winter paints on its bleak, leaning timbers.
No smoke curl charms the view or adds warmth.

Inside, a very old woman waits, rocking
to a song with no words or music, remembering.
Neither joyful nor sad, she numbly endures
the repetition of years and seasons.

If she lives until spring, she will emerge
much like her tulips urged by the warmth.
Her gnarled hands and rusty coffee cans
will water every living thing, tear away dry vines,
expose new shoots to sun and rain.

She will be about her garden until autumn frosts
shrivel the blossoms and chill her ancient bones.
Then she will shut the door of her tiny fortress,
remain unseen like the tubers sleeping in her garden.
She will care little for passing strangers who gape
and wonder how the little house still stands.

36 Hours

We saw the doe first,
emerging from the woods.
Our bedroom frames her regal pose, tawny
rippling muscles, eyes wary.
She quietly moves forward, turns
her proud head back—a signal.
We crouch behind the curtain
just as the first fawn
wobbles into view, followed quickly
by another baby, somewhat smaller.
Mother doe keeps them there a few
seconds more. We hold our breath.
Slowly she passes beyond our garden,
moves forward, turning
at the road, leading the tentative twins
into the safety of the dense woods.
Your arms circle my waist, and you say,
"How beautiful."

This morning, almost the same time,
the doe slides past our window again.
We quickly spot the larger fawn
following a few feet behind,
leaving a void.

Later we hear a workman found,
near the edge of the woods, a fawn
curled perfectly still and cold. You say,
"It must have been weak; this was
Nature's way." I touch my stomach,
remember the tiny life I never got to hold.

That Spring

Walking the dusty gravel road from school,
the air hung heavily, too hot for March.
My thin-soled shoes felt the rocks
as I counted fence posts and prayed
our neighbor had tied up his dog.
His bare-toothed growls, piercing barks,
often set my skinny legs flying.

Arriving home, hunger led a path
to the kitchen and Grandma. Hearing
conversation in the living room escalating
into a passionate argument between
adult siblings, I questioned Grandma.

"It's the bad air," she told me.
"It's been wrong all day.
Folks' nerves are raw. Lord knows
we need some rain to clean it up."

That night, just as Mama leaned
to tuck me and sister in, she raised up,
listening to the puffing of a freight train.
"It didn't whistle at the crossing," she cried.
"Get up, girls! God help us, it's a tornado!"

Our family gathered tight in the hall, arms
clutching each other, as the house moaned.
In tears, Aunt Isobel held fast to brother Ed.
I remember eerie green lightning, a roar
so terrible we never heard our five pines fall.
Terrified, I fell to my knees at Mama's feet,
prayed right out loud, "Jesus save us!"

And Mama said, later, that's why he did.

Crossing Lines

Daddy's rattletrap paint truck pulled up
in front of the drab, peeling house—
my home, not his. He lived across town
with his other family, but today would
be different, a day for just me.
On this golden morning he came, hurrying
to take me to the 1947 Louisiana State Fair.
He kept the motor running as I jumped in,
full of happiness, champagne uncorked,
the battered old truck a Cinderella carriage.
Daddy, grizzled, unkempt, whisked me away.

The fairgrounds teemed with the smells
of corn dogs, cotton candy and funnel cakes.
I waited for Daddy to buy tickets, legs taut,
set for the dash to the gate—hurry, hurry!
Then I heard his raucous laughter and ran
to his side. "It's Colored People's Day!"

He saw the disappointment on my face.
"You wanna go anyway?" Behind the window,
the black man offered two tickets, saying,
"But you and the chile is welcome."

So we went in to the happy fray, greeted by
smiling faces at every turn. We soared on
the ferris wheel, the merry-go-round, glimpsed
the hoochie-coochie girls, their sepia hips
gyrating to the rhythmic beat, beat, beat.
I watched, big-eyed, Daddy's hand tight on mine.

We stayed all day. I was happy beyond telling.
As he drove slowly back to my house, Daddy said,
"Those people didn't mind us being there at all."

Miss Edna

I remember 3rd and 4th grades in
gray scale, with little or no color
cheering Miss Edna's domain.
She ruled supreme, teaching both grades
in the same dull room. Her few resources
were dog-eared books, chalk and blackboard.

A maiden lady of a certain age with
little or no hope of marriage, I believe
she maintained a stern facade, cautious
a tender heart might be discovered
beneath the stiff-collared blouse.

She guarded a small cupboard filled
with ear oil, cotton and unguents.
She warmed the ear oil in a jar lid
set off to the side of the pot-bellied
stove. A Balm in Gilead for
childhood earaches.

A small, locked drawer held a cache of
Smith Brothers licorice cough drops.
Craving anything sweet,
we coughed our heads off to get one.

My older sister vexed Miss Edna no end,
wiggling and tossing her curls at Henry,
her 4th-grade freckled slave.
One day, however, when sister's hand
waved for a trip to the privy, Miss Edna
turned and wrote long at the blackboard.
Sister got so angry, she wet the floor.

Miss Edna handed Henry the mop.

Near the Fishing Pier

An island woman lies
on top of a weathered picnic table.
An opened newspaper shades her face.
Sun-burnished arms rest loosely;
crooked fingers open, relaxed in sleep.
Bunions poke holes in her faded sneakers.

The breeze from the Sound lifts
the hem of her shirt, lets it fall,
repeats the quiet pattern, lifting, falling,
in breathing rhythm.
She is island-rooted with the live oaks.

How long must I remain a stranger here?
Walk how far on yielding sand? Watch in awe
how many shimmering sunsets, or feast enough
on blue crabs, brown shrimp and the disoriented
flounders that stray into my tattered drop-nets?

When I have steeped bones,
flesh and soul enough,
in sand and salty waves; when
my heart cries, "I can offer no more!"—

perhaps then I will have earned the right
to make my bed an old picnic table;
there, rocked by tide, wind and buoy's clang,
fall asleep on warm wooden cushions.

No Trespassing

One day a home that sheltered me
self destructed—old wiring, they said.
In truth, for years, my stepdad had been
jumping the meter with cable wires.
Though no one said a word, I remember
Mama's oft-repeated prediction:
"You'll burn the house down one day."

The meter was on the enclosed back porch,
hung high above our noisy refrigerator.
We knew the time of month
the meter man came around.
We kids knew to keep a sharp eye out,
give warning in plenty of time.

Mama wouldn't have allowed it,
but I knew which clamps to squeeze.
I knew how to release the jumper cable,
the one that slowed the whirling
meter, and kept the bill so low.
Skinny, scared young girl that I was,
thank God, I never had to do it.

After the fire, a small, low-roofed house
was built, a house that never settled in.
Returning after 40 years, it still looks transient.
How can a picture in the mind's album
be ripped out and replaced so quickly?
I want to peel off and tear to bits this trespasser
set askew upon the roots of my home.

Tar Foot Morning

Rising at 7:00 a.m., I put my arm
in the wrong sleeve of my
soft flannel robe, untangle,
and slipper-stumble to the bathroom.
I have to be someplace this morning.

Lifting my toothbrush to clean
fuzzy teeth, I hear a cardinal
chirping and look out.
He sounds close by. Ah, there he is,
perched among white rhododendrons.
Oh, Lord, I've got to keep moving.

What to eat? Nothing complicated,
I have to be someplace this morning.
Holding coffee, milky and sweet, my
hands are warm. Drawn to the porch,
I see the clematis vine bloomed overnight.
Somewhere, a sweet shrub perfumes the air.

Nibbling on a cold croissant, I watch
thieving squirrels eying the bird feeder.
I ask the sun to linger, coax out
morning glory seeds, nudge phlox awake.
The cool morning teems with life and promise.
Why do I have to be someplace this morning?

My feet won't move voluntarily;
they must be willed, pulled away from here.
Though I want to throw open windows, invite
wood fairies in to dance, whirl
in my soft robe until I'm spent—I can't.
I have to be someplace this morning.

Thou Shalt Not

Is it right
to rearrange our memories?

I hear it in the tall tales
told at family reunions.
There is much to learn when
middle-aged children reveal
secrets they got away with
right under unsuspecting eyes.

It is tempting to correct a tale
that takes a foreign direction
but if a small lie seems plausible,
forces a glum uncle to choke
with laughter, spraying
an amber stain of minted tea
on Prissy Asbell's crisp white blouse,

is it not worth the risk of Hell
for such a moment sublime?

Miz Lucille

Our next-door neighbor met us with apples
on day two of our vacation in the mountains.
Miz Lucille came right on in.
Tall, with wide hips and shoulders to match,
she planted herself solidly before us.

She said she was 83, plowed
the whole mountain all her life because
her old man was sorry, mostly sat
by the fire with his pipe. She said
he died some 25 years back.
She smiled a toothless grin, then added,
"But Amos is a dandy, he can fix anything.

He's fixed my porch, planted my garden—
why, he can even cook. He's a little
young for me, though." She rubbed a large
black mole on her cheek. "I believe in
miracles, and I've set about praying
for this black mole to disappear."
She smiled, "I don't think Amos minds, but..."

Miz Lucille claimed God gave her
superhuman strength. She straightaway
picked my friend right up off the floor,
started for her husband, but he raised
his hands in protest. She said she believed in
the power of prayer and was praying hard
to grow a third set of teeth because,
she affirmed, "Amos is a dandy."

The following day, I climbed her porch,
with sketch pad and easel in tow—
despite the smell of cat food, burned collards
in a room warmed to 90 degrees, despite old cats

slithering in and out my legs, the likeness came.
Miz Lucille thought it made her look old.

We had just five days, time enough to burn
memories of clean air and crisp mountain apples
freely given by an ageless mountain woman
brave enough to live alone as she pleases
and to love foolishly if she chooses.
On the last day I learned from her daughter,

Amos was 43.

Portraits from Life

Likenesses can be made with
a camera, but I would not see
your mind, working behind
your eyes, to see mine.

When we part, each of us will
take away a sketch of the other.

If we share the small space of
conversation, we reveal ourselves
in three dimensions.

Something about your manner—or
the way you lean in when you speak—
stirs the pigment, dips the brush,
as memory paints and files you away.

I would not risk a touch.
Your eye has already spied
my crooked tooth, my nose and dark hair,
the soft contours of my breasts.

Our minds collect canvasses.
We offer palettes for others to paint.

Painting flesh in shadow takes skill;
true colors are more wisely chosen
in morning's honest light.
Still, something of you will remain.

Mirror Image

The automatic door opens,
the last help offered. She struggles
with cumbersome bags of groceries.
I feel the weight of the bags, know
her stiff muscles as she takes
the ponderous steps to her SUV.
Opening the back doors, she loads
the bags, nestling the eggs carefully
against the bread for cushioning.

She is my age, about my size, repeating
the endless ritual of buying groceries.
Don't tell the bride how often
she will repeat this thankless task,
how many times she will stare numbly
upon a pale carcass of poultry, wondering
if it might jump in a pan and cook itself.
She would not believe you.

Exhaustion and futility paint
a dull mask on the woman's face.
I am in her skin, her thoughts, mine.
"Just for a while, Lord, let me live
in a nice hotel, with a deep tub,
Room Service—and no kitchen."

At last, she flings the door shut and,
with a sigh, climbs in the driver's seat.
The parking space in front of her is open.
I am guessing she will save the effort
of backing out. Sure enough,
she drives through, betting no one
pulls in at the same moment. As she
leaves, she guns the engine—just a bit.
Under my breath, I say, "You go, Girl!"

At Whispering Pines Campground

In this photo, I stand at the edge
of a small trout stream, casting line,
allowing the corn-baited hook to drift.
The water slips by, unconcerned.
It only brings the fish man feeds it.
Left alone, it merely flows downstream.

Still, I look content, as water carries
my small burdens along, cleanses
the wastes of my useless worries,
clears my ears to hear its gentle sound.
To flow downstream is its purpose.
There is healing in a mountain stream.

The Voyeur

Half-dressed, I sit on the side of the bed
watching the lone Robin outside my window.
He seems almost within arm's reach, scratching,
up to his knobby knees in dew-soaked grass.
Bowing his head, he turns an ear, listening
patiently for Worm to make the wrong move.

The window and tree shadow hide my human form,
muffle the sound of my involuntary breathing.
He sets mind to task, unaware of prying eyes.
Now, he looks up, but I remain still.
Soon he returns to his breakfast foraging.

Here we are together, Bird.
You do not ponder religious philosophy
this Sunday morning, yet you appear content,
in no hurry to sing your praises.
You have all morning to poke and piddle around,
scratching, talking to yourself.
Your feathers look perfectly pressed.

Grandma would say the Devil is here,
sitting on my lap, keeping me idle
watching you, Robin. What do you think?
I prefer to believe the Creator gave
this gift of you—to me.

You jump at the sound of a horn.
I cannot watch you longer, for
I must heed the call of Husband waiting
with motor running to whisk me off to sermon
and song, where I shall be tortured long
by self-righteous underwear and pinch-toe shoes.

The Whisperers

Ghosts wander freely through my house:
Grandmama and Mama, sometimes
the Aunts. They spend more time
in my kitchen than anywhere else.
Grandmama moves often into my apron
and makes biscuits. Mama reminds me
from the cupboard to use unsweetened
cornbread in the dressing, stirs in a bit
of soda just before pouring it into the hot
iron skillet. Aunt Isobel stops my
hand at the stove dial, insisting her
pound cake starts in a cold oven.

I candy the sweet potatoes according to
Great-Grandma Dora; let my dough
rest 4 days in the refrigerator,
the secret of Aunt Nell's light rolls.
Chopped eggs are added to Mama's
giblet gravy, while the turkey roasts in
an island of dressing, her way.

As I measure the 2 cups flour for pastry,
I add an extra half teaspoon of salt to
the recipe, a trick I've taught my daughters;
adding another small tradition to those
that will be passed on by the loving ghosts
who live in my house, especially the kitchen.

Evening Rounds

We leave supper dishes behind, pulled outside
by the scent of Narcissus in the soft breeze.
As we inspect our springtime garden,
the scent of nature's harmony is everywhere.
As Narcissus fades, Rose will unfold her petals;
a headier scent will fill the garden, bidding me
risk thorns, bleed willingly, for one perfect bud.
For now, I bless these brave spring bloomers.

Thoughtful Creeping Vinca spreads her
lavender blankets over naked tree roots.
Leaning to touch tiny Lily of the Valley bells,
I am startled by the abrupt roar of an ATV
entering the woods nearby.

The sudden discord interrupts peaceful birdsong,
distracts the eye resting gently on sunset splendor.
The noise persists; we choose to surrender.
Making our way indoors, I pause to console
my Daffodils, unable to lift petal petticoats—
and *flee*.

Polished Jewels

Artists search their palettes, unable to
capture Fall's jewel tones, elusive
deep shadows, the kiss of sun.
Fall will not stand still to pose, moves
about, draping jeweled necklaces
on crooked dogwoods, stretching
to crown the mountains.

Hills put on their Fall attire slowly,
choosing to tantalize: revealing first
rusty reds, then blurs of topaz and amber.
Sapphire and ruby appear with patience,
colors of crusty, rough stones.

Her random decor is not unflawed,
but when only tall pines and hemlock
thrust cold arms toward dull winter skies
and stark tree skeletons stand in snow,
we will tumble over in sweet memory
Fall's rough stone colors
until all become polished jewels,
perfect, and warm to the touch.

The Party's Over

The mountains wait, stone
silent, for Fall to go about her business,
then depart.

The hills grow weary of the gaudy
season's riot and wait for Winter's
housekeeping to blow rattling
crumbs of faded leaves
down to valleys below.

As beauty longs to remove
makeup, retreat from admiration,
the mountains yearn to pull up
snowy blankets and sleep
a dreamless Winter, having set
the precocious alarm clock of Spring.

Season Change

Catching my breath, I lean on
my hoe and study the small plot.
I sense the soil is still healthy;
there is time enough to scratch out
a small fall garden.
I am betting the plants will set roots
before the first killing frost,
a splash of green holding
a feeble hand against winter.

I feel the grit, hurry in for a hot shower.
I glimpse my nakedness in the mirror.
The mist does not conceal spider veins,
sagging flesh.

I dress and brush my graying hair.
A little color on mouth and cheeks
completes the ritual.
I turn back again to face
the full-length mirror. Defiant, I
place my strong hand hard against the glass
and feel a chill.

Continuity

Perhaps when my daughter remembers
today, she'll recall the laughter shared,
the cup of coffee she kept spilling,
as she flitted about, seeing to my needs.
I hear my voice coming from her mouth.

She wants to help, her heart so generous.
Life demands so much of her,
I feel guilty, stealing her time.
Surgery put this arm in a sling, resting.
Is there a sling to rest my child somehow?

She shampooed my hair in the shower, washed
my back and checked out the wound site.
Clucking like a hen, she gently dried me off.
"Funny YOU giving me a bath, sweetheart," I said.
"Well, how many times have you bathed me?" she said.

Her answer echoed a conversation
I had years ago as Mother's life wound down.
I remember a black mole on her back
as I bathed her, the terrible burn scar on her leg.
"I know you are tired, sweetheart;
 I hate being a burden on you," she said.

"Well, how many times have you bathed me?" I said.

Sitting on the Side of the Bed

He loves the morning as I do
in our sacred bedroom,
before the phone rings,
before we must dress,
when sleepiness still slows
our movements. We put off
thoughts of the day ahead,
sitting on the side of the bed.

He shuffles off to get coffee;
I raise the blind to the view,
pull sheet and quilt over pillows,
smoothing out the side of the bed.

The room welcomes our waking.
We're rested and happy here,
sharing secrets, facing problems,
sitting close on the side of the bed.

Mama says it ruins the mattress
if you sit on the side of the bed.
I used to feel guilt, but no more.
No, I would not trade this splendid hour
for a perfect mattress, unspoiled,
putting off thoughts of the day ahead,
sitting here on the side of the bed.

Feeding the Soul

Today you lay beside me, studying
the patterns on the stippled ceiling.
One arm drapes your forehead,
shades your eyes. My head rests
in the crook of the other.
You say,

"What happens when we die, I wonder?
Isn't it possible that death erases
all memory, just as we cannot remember
anything before our birth?

If I died first, and could still remember today,
the way your body temperature matches
mine exactly, remember
your scent and taste, remember,

but, unable to reach out and hold you—
I'd prefer the nothingness before my life began."

Your words floated above us
until I drew them in,
opened my heart and received
nourishment,

enough for this life—
until you find me in the next.

Enough

The gravel crunches under the tires
as he leaves for church. I am left
behind, a coughing, red-nosed outcast.

"Now, you just rest and try to get well,"
he said before he left. His concern
is real, my suffering his.
It is like that now.

When he mows the lawn, my stomach knots
if he comes too close to the ditch,
if his face looks too flushed from the heat.

Nursing a second cup of coffee, I recall
wartime partings, letters, phone calls—
never enough. Children years, demanding,
often divided, often multiplied, happiness.
A pilot's plane was his mistress, my earthbound
dreams poor competition for such a siren.

It was never enough.

At last we are back to our beginnings,
having found each other again without
road map or compass. We stumbled
on wrong paths, but miraculously tethers bound
by young love's passion held fast.

I hear the gravel crunch. My pulse quickens
as he returns. The familiar walk and
gentle face set my life in motion, define
my existence. As he yanks off his tie, collapses
in his chair, I know this is his haven, as it is mine.

It is enough.

Washing

Lazily, I wash the juice glasses, rinse
away generous suds, look closely
for traces of lipstick, and move on
in the natural way, cleanest first.

The water very warm, soap slippery,
soothes arthritic hands.
The task is over too soon,
so little to wash:
two cups, two plates,
breakfast dishes for two
taking my time.

How pleasant
to wash
for two.

How numbing
to wash for one.

Returning

Winding down Blood Mountain,
I could not find
remembered rivulets chasing, tumbling
down the old mountain, seeking out
the creeks, hurrying, frothing
to meet sister streams pushing north.
Today, at the wide curve, the stone fountain stands dry.

Relentless drought has denied the mountain waterfalls,
denied all things wild, hardened the heart to forget.
Springtime stops along a ridge where I touched
plump laurel buds, watched diamond fire light up
rain drops on tiny wild iris blooms and spider webs.
Today, I open the window at a familiar spot and listen
for gurgling mountain brooks, but hear nothing.

At Cleveland, fat drops pelt the windshield and trace
muddy squiggles on the dusty hood. I scarcely hope
for more than a passing shower, a fickle teaser, destined
to disappoint the mountain forests to the north; poplars,
pines and firs that shadow hiding places of thirsty
deer, black bear and their young; secretive wild things
that come to drink from mountain creeks and waterfalls.

I start my journey home. Once more,
I drive north through beauty both natural and mysterious.
The sun blazes, but gushing gutters attest to a heavy rain.
Arriving at Turner's Corners, Bogg's Creek churns.
With each ascending curve, my heart lightens.
There, across a divide, I see two triumphant waterfalls.
I hear again the liquid music of the mountains.

Acknowledgments

My special gratitude goes to Robert S. King for his patience and expertise in framing this, my first chapbook. Also, I want to thank Diane Kistner for her help in the cover design.

Without the encouragement and love of my friend and mentor, Nancy Simpson, these poems would never have come together in a collection. When a writer and teacher of Nancy's caliber says, "You are a writer," it is most humbling. I hope these poems will bring credit to her faith in me.

My gratitude also goes to the members of the North Carolina Writers' Network West, the Shallow Enders Critique Group, and the Georgia Poetry Society for their support. The works of Janice Moore, Glenda Beall, Mary Ricketson, Glenda Barrett, Robert S. King, and Robert W. Kimsey are just a few of the many wonderful poets whose words sing in my ears.

Best of all has been the support and enduring love of my husband, Norm, and my precious family. This includes my dear "sister," Barbara Groce.

Much gratitude goes to those publishers who kept me encouraged by accepting my poems for their publications.

A Sense of Place: "The House of Cards"
DAR American Heritage National Contest 2nd Place Poetry Winner:
    "The Whisperers"
Echoes Across the Blue Ridge: "Returning"
Women's Spaces, Women's Places: "Tar Foot Morning"
Wild Goose Poetry Review: "36 Hours," "The Party's Over"
FutureCycle 2011: "Season Change"

Cover painting and interior graphic of "Miz Lucille" by Carole Richard Thompson; photo of the author by Norm Thompson; cover and interior book design by Diane Kistner (dkistner@futurecycle.org); text and titling, Adobe Garamond

About FutureCycle Press

FutureCycle Press is dedicated to publishing lasting English-language poetry and flash fiction books, chapbooks, and anthologies in both print-on-demand and ebook formats. Founded in 2007 by long-time independent editor/publishers and partners Diane Kistner and Robert S. King, the press incorporated as a nonprofit in 2012. A number of our editors are distinguished poets and authors in their own right, and we have been actively involved in the small press movement going back to the early seventies.

The FutureCycle Poetry Book Prize and honorarium is awarded annually for the best full-length volume of poetry we publish in a calendar year. Introduced in 2013, our Good Works projects are devoted to issues of global significance, with all proceeds donated to a related worthy cause. We are dedicated to giving all authors we publish the care their work deserves, making our catalog of titles the most distinguished it can be, and paying forward any earnings to fund more great books.

We've learned a few things about independent publishing over the years. We've also evolved a unique, resilient publishing model that allows us to focus mainly on vetting and preserving for posterity the most books of exceptional quality without becoming overwhelmed with bookkeeping and mailing, fundraising activities, or taxing editorial and production "bubbles." To find out more about what we are doing, come see us at www.futurecycle.org.

www.ingramcontent.com/pod-product-compliance
Lightning Source LLC
Chambersburg PA
CBHW061200040426
42445CB00013B/1764